The Language of Love

Benjamin Osei Kuffour JNR

Acknowledgements

I wish to acknowledge, first of all, God for giving me the wisdom to write, opening my eyes to the Scriptures to understand and granting me unremitting devotion to the things I wanted to see happen. They have all come to fruition. I wish to express my heartfelt thanks and appreciation to Rev. Bill Vincent, my publisher of Revival Waves Ministry who made a deliberate effort and choice to help me publish manuscripts I have written and compiled. May God elevate you to a city set on a hill so that everybody will see and marvel at the works you have produced. Only those that risk going too far find out how far they can go.

Secondly, I wish to appreciate and affirm my mother, Mrs. Christiana Osei Kuffour for encouraging me, Pamela Edusei Ankisiwai for affirming, believing and encouraging me when she barely knew me. I say, *Merci infiniment et que Le Dieu vous bénisse abondamment!!!*

I wish to express my thanks to Asante Elvis, Nii Clement Aryee and his older sister for reading The Language of Love before it was finally published and giving me ideas and opinions which were very informative. I am really grateful.

Thank you, dear reader for purchasing The Language of Love. This book is very informative, in my estimation, as it will provide wisdom nuggets to you. I pray and hope that all and sundry are addressed in this book. Thank you once again and God bless you!!!

Introduction

It is very interesting to see people fall in love and then later fall out of love. Sometimes they fall out of love with the same intensity that they fell into love. Love is very powerful; it is a very strong thing.

Love is shown or expressed both in the presence and the absence of someone. If you love your wife, tell her, help her in the kitchen and communicate with her. Tell her what you go through at work, church, family meetings.

Everybody wants to learn the language of love. You want to be able to communicate with the language of love. There is a sentiment in Psalm 120:5-7 that is expressed by the Psalmist which, I think, describes the communication problem. Each one of us has good intentions to communicate but sometimes when we communicate, it does not come out the way we want it to come out. So this is what the Psalmist says, *"Woe is me, that I dwell in Meshech, that I dwell among the tents of Kedar! My soul has dwelt too long with one who hates peace. I am for peace; but when I speak, they are for war."*

I consider this the challenge of communication. **Three ideas** are expressed by the writer of this Psalm.

The first one describes **where he stays and he talks about the environment he stays in.** He says that the environment was very, very war-like and it has affected him. Sometimes when you stay in a place of war, strife, arguments and fights, it affects you.

For example, if you grew up in an environment where there was always chaos and no love, eventually it affects you.

You learn language, habits and communication that reflects where you live. So the Psalmist says, *"Woe to me because of where I dwell."* Where he lived. Where he grew up. The environment he was in. When we talk about the language of love, it is always important to examine the environment we grew up in. If you grew up in an environment where insults are like conversation. It happens like that. People insult people without any consideration. *"Oh, get away from there."* It is the normal language.

In that environment, you pick up the same language and if you get into marriage with that, you may find yourself throwing out words that are very destructive. The writer said he was affected by the language of the environment he was living in.

The second thing that I want to bring to your attention is that he said *"because of that I like it but when I speak, it produces war."* **He talks about his inability to truly express the intents of his heart.** When it comes to matters of love, you can find somebody who is in love but does not know how to say it. Sometimes you can find a husband who loves his wife dearly but he cannot speak words of love and when he speaks, it becomes a quarrel.

The wife loves the husband so much when she opens her mouth, the love language comes like an insult. Even speaking love comes like a criticism because if you grew up in a place where your mother insulted you, it was a sign of endearment. She loves you and said, *"Oh, look at your big head. Get away."* That is the way of telling you *"I like you."* Some of us grew up in environments like that. *"Oh, look at your big leg."* It means she likes you.

Her intent is to say, *"I love you"* but the language is *"Look at your big head."* So she is for peace but what she is speaking is not for peace. She is for love; what she is speaking is not love. So the writer here says, *"I want to speak peace but anytime I speak, there is war."* That is the second thing.

The third thing is that **because he also lives among people who are always fighting even when the word he speaks is love it becomes war.** A lot of marriages and relationships are like that. You find two people who truly love each other but they cannot stand each other in a room for five minutes. They start a conversation, by the time it moves beyond Sule Muntari, the Black Stars and they are now talking about their lives, there is trouble.

They have to start arguing even if they talk about Black Stars, they have to argue. *"Yes, it is Sule Muntari." "No, it is Aminu Dramani."* The whole conversation started very nicely but within five minutes, it has deteriorated, then you argue and leave. If you love each other and want to come back, the moment you are together, after five minutes of conversation, you are back to quarrelling again. You love but you cannot communicate love.

Proverbs 21:9 declares, *"Better to dwell in the corner of a housetop, than in a house shared with a contentious woman."* Interesting verse, is it not? It is better to dwell in the corner of a housetop. Now, a house top, for what I know, is like the rooftop and the Bible says, *"It is better to go to the rooftop and hide in a corner than to live in a big mansion with a contentious woman."*

Before the men will rejoice, go to Proverbs 26:21, *"As charcoal is to burning coals, and wood to fire, so is a contentious man to kindle strife."* The equation is balanced. It simply means both man and woman can be contentious. **When somebody is contentious, it means the person hits up a point and uses it against another. Somebody who enters into a fight or engages in a fight and when the Bible describes a person as contentious, it means the person always wants to fight even when they want to show affection, it looks as if they are fighting.**

Their words always have something in it that is striking somebody. Their thoughts are always fighting somebody. They can be together in a relationship with somebody – a husband or a wife – but it is like a fight. They want to win and that is a contentious person. **If he is a man, the Bible says he is like fire burning wood. If she is a woman, it is better to go and live at the roof than with her.**

So the bottom line is that contention is not good in a relationship and all of us know contention is not good but once in a while we become contentious and we get so contentious and heated that we destroy the relationship we love or the person we love.

The sad thing is that after we have destroyed the person we love, we want to go back and then we go back to destroy it again. In our hearts, we want to love, we want the relationship to work but anytime we are together, there is a fight and there are relationships like that.

Sometimes it is a boyfriend, girlfriend, fiancé, fiancée. You meet somebody you want to marry. The two of you really believe that you can marry each other but too much fight.

Sometimes you manage to go through but every day is a fight. Every issue is a fight – the children are a fight, the parents are a fight, the house help is a fight, the food is a fight, the TV is a fight. The telephone is a fight. *"Why did you put the phone there? It is not supposed to be there."*

The soap is a fight. Towels is a fight. Water is a fight. Bucket is a fight. You fight over everything. Sometimes when you see that happening, you begin to ask, *"If they love each other so much, why did they marry?"* So we have to learn how to communicate. How many of you really sometimes feel you love somebody but you just cannot get along with the person? Have you had that experience before?

What is a positive language? Let us go to Genesis 2:23. **In Genesis 2:23, we learn a few things about the positive language of love and the first person who spoke those words was Adam when Eve was brought to him as his wife. He had not met this girl before but he meets this girl and this is what he said.**

Adam said, *"This is now bone of my bones and flesh of my flesh; she shall be called Woman, because she was taken out of Man."* **This is bone of my bones and flesh of my flesh. This was the first positive language.**

The second positive language that you will find in a relationship is not a husband and wife situation. I think it speaks to all of us - Ruth 1:16-17.

When Naomi began to tell Ruth to go back because Naomi was returning to her people and Ruth had lost her husband (Naomi's son) and she wanted to conjoin her mother-in-law back to her people. Naomi said no and Ruth spoke these words:

"But Ruth said, 'Entreat me not to leave you, or to turn back from following after you; for wherever you go, I will go; and wherever you lodge, I will lodge; your people shall be my people, and your God, my God. Where you die, I will die, and there will I be buried. The LORD do so to me, and more also, if anything but death parts you and me.' "

In a sense what Ruth was saying was what Adam said. *"You are the bone of my bones. You are the flesh of my flesh. Where you will go, I will go. Your God will be my God. I will die where you die and woe to me if anything except death separates us."* **We captured these words and made them part of our wedding vows in church because they express the true language of love.**

I am going to walk you through **five love languages.** I got the idea from a book - the 5 languages of love by Gary Chapman. If you find that book, read it. It is going to help you to know how to master the language of love.

Some people have been upset by the popularity of this slogan, and I have seen them try to counter with the sticker, "Love Happens." Actually, they have it wrong. Shit *does* happen. But love does not. Love does not happen all by itself. Love is created.

In his stirring book *Son Rise*, Barry Neil Kaufman tells an astonishing true story of how he and his wife healed their once-autistic son and helped nurture him to a happy, extroverted life. Kaufman and his wife made a conscious choice to see their son's disability as a great blessing to them. It was just a choice, like choosing to face the sun instead of facing your shadows. The way we choose to see the world creates the world we see.

Contents

Chapter One

AFFIRMATION

The first language of love is **the language of affirmation.** That was Adam's words. When he said, *"This is now bone of my bones and flesh of my flesh."* That is what Ruth meant when she said, *"Do not let me depart from you. Where you go, that is where I am going to be."* It is affirmation. What is an affirmation?

An affirmation is a declaration or statement of support and endorsement. When you say, *"You affirm somebody"* **it means you support the affirmed person. You make the person strong and stand firm.** You affirm them and the first language of love is the language of affirmation. **It is speaking words to make somebody feel empowered, encouraged and uplifted.**

In any relationship where there is husband and wife or two people who want to marry, two people who meet each other, they get attracted to each other, they like how the other person looks. *"I like your hairstyle."* *"I like his shirt."* So they want to get close. **The first thing that you do in order to show that you love the person is to speak words of affirmation.**

Can you imagine what will happen if you meet this girl, you like the girl, you really love her, you really want to know her more and you tell her, *"I do not like your hairstyle?"* That is the first thing you said to her when you met her. *"I do not like your hairstyle." "I do not like the way you are."* Do you think the relationship will go any further? No. That will be the end of the relationship. When Eve was presented to Adam, Adam did not say, *"Ah, what is this?"* No because he had not seen her before. He could have condemned her and said, *"Ah, she is not strong. Look at her"* and criticized how she looked and I am sure he could have criticized. He said, *"This is now bone of my bones and flesh of my flesh."* **It is the word of affirmation.**

If you are going to grow in love, your marriage is going to grow, you have to learn the language of affirmation. For example, you should be able to tell the person you love, *"You are the best gift God has given to me."* Affirm the person and it is not difficult, is it? What are the words you use when you want to court people? One of the things I like about Adam, even after Eve had gotten them into trouble, Adam said, *"The woman You gave me…"*

In a sense you can say she is to blame but also he was not shifting blame. He was still acknowledging, *"This woman is God's gift to me. We are in a mess but I believe she came from God."* It is affirmation. *"The woman You gave me…"* is an affirmation. **Every good and perfect gift comes from God.** He was saying, *"Yes, we are in a mess but I still believe this woman came from God."* That is so important. **That affirmation is so important because many times when relationships get into trouble instead of saying words of affirmation, we say words of disowner ship.**

"I should not have married you." "I have made a mistake." But Adam said, *"The woman you gave me…"* **Affirmation.** *"This is bone of my bones and flesh of my flesh." "You are the best gift God gave to me."* **That language must be learnt because sometimes the person you are married to does not look like the best gift from**

God. They look like the worst gift of God. As if God went to Heaven, into the storeroom, searched the storeroom, finished and said, *"Michael, is there anything left?"* Michael says, *"Yes, in the valley there, there is another storeroom."* God goes there to search there as well and finds a man.

He is hiding in a corner. He is dusty. He is in a bad state and God says, *"This is the one. I am going to give him to Sister Mary."* **Sometimes when you marry and you look at the person you have married, they do not look like the one from God but it is an affirmation. Death and life are in the power of the tongue.** You get what you say. If you say your wife is a tiger, she will be a tiger. If you say your husband is wicked, he will be wicked. If you say he does not know how to love, he will never know how to love. If you want it, say it. **Just as we confess the Word of God as we receive the miracle, you must confess words of affirmation for you to receive what you are believing for.** Your husband and wife will never become anything beyond who you say they are. If you say they are good, they will be good. If you say they are troublesome, they will be troublesome. Death and life are in the power of the tongue. So you must be able to say, *"You are the best gift from God to me. I like your hairstyle."*

Every man should be able to say that. The woman should be able to say that. *"I like your cloths. I like your shoes. I like the way you are dressed when you wear your tie."* **They are words of affirmation because if you love somebody, you are not going to tear the person down. You are going to strengthen the person.** Words of affirmation emphasize on **three things:**

♥ They emphasize on **the worth of the person. The value of the person. The person is valuable.** So when you are speaking words, you must ask yourself, *"Are these words I am* *speaking focusing on the worth of the person or devaluing the person?"*

♥ It must, secondly, focus on **the contribution of the person.** Even if they are doing what they normally do, you must be able to appreciate it. For example, if your wife cooks, you must be able to appreciate that contribution. If your husband pays the children's school fees, you must be able to appreciate that contribution and you must verbalize it. **Do not take for granted what each one of you does for the other person because one of the dangers of every relationship especially marriage relationships is when we take each other's contribution for granted.**

When you say, *"Well, it is your job anyway. You should be doing it. You are the man."* or *"After all, you are the woman. It is your job. You have cooked and so what? Are you not a woman?"* Yes, traditionally, you may say, *"She is supposed to do it"* but it takes effort to do it. You cannot take anything for granted. Wives, do not take your husband's contribution for granted and husbands, do not take your wife's contribution for granted. So you focus on the worth. Secondly, you focus on contribution.

♥ Thirdly, you focus on **significance. The person is significant. They are important. They are valuable. They are vital to you. Language of significance.** When a pastor stands before his congregation to speak about his wife, he is affirming his wife publicly. That is what he does and he does it deliberately because he wants everybody to see it. He is the pastor of his church and he wants his congregation to see how it is done. It is deliberate.

When his wife organizes an event and he comes to praise her, he is not saying his wife is better than all the other women but he just wants every man in his church to know *"You do not take for granted what your wife does"* and women, do not take for granted what your husband does too. **Her contribution may be little but affirm it. Speak well of it. Support it. Endorse it. Stand by it. Do not tear it down. Do not compare it to somebody else. Do not minimize it and devalue it.**

It is very easy to do that because in this world, there will be somebody who is better than the person you have married, who does something better, who knows better, who looks more beautiful, more handsome, who knows how to cook better and who has more money. There will always be somebody like that. Even somebody is more handsome than the richest man in the world. He cannot buy handsomeness. It is a commodity he does not have. So everybody lacks something and the saddest point in any relationship is that somebody bypasses all these things and only focuses on the negative. That is not affirmation and it applies to both men and women.

You say *Amen* when it suits you. Ask yourself whether you are also affirming. So that is the first language of love which is the language of affirmation. When we feel like saying something that is not affirming, hold your mouth and leave your room. Check yourself because if you have lived in an environment where there was insult, you will insult your partner. In my family where I grew up, we did not insult anybody. Never. I do not remember insulting. My mother will beat me. My father will beat me but they will not insult me.

So when I grew up, when it comes to insult, I do not know how to insult. There are people who are masters of insult. They have the vocabularies and the adjectives. When I hear people insult, I marvel. How did they learn that? I do not know some of the words they use. There are some words I do not use. They are not in my vocabulary. It was never part of my vocabulary when I was growing up. **So if you grew up in an environment where people insulted, I cannot blame you but I will blame you when you grow up as an adult and you do not learn to polish your language because then you have power over what you do. You have a choice and you can control what you do.**

Chapter Two

QUALITY TIME

Second language of love is expressed in **quality time**. What is quality time? **Quality time is committing time to something important. You can always tell how much a person loves you by how much time the person sacrifices to be with you. I am not talking about how much time the person has for you but how much time they sacrifice. For the time to be quality, it has to have opportunity cost and it has to compete with something. Then you can say it is quality time.** If, for example, the Black Stars are playing a match with Nigeria. I am watching the match with my wife. We are together watching TV.

She wants to start a conversation but I am watching Michael Essien. We are spending time together because there is time and we are together but it is not quality time. **Quality time is not just being with somebody. Quality time is taking your attention from something important and focusing it on the person you love.** So if you switch on the TV just before a free kick, turn off the TV and say, *"Ok, sweetheart. Let us talk"* **that is quality time.**

I know the scene I described probably will never happen in Ghana. When there is a free kick and the ball is going to be kicked, your wife says to you, *"I want to discuss something with you."* You will say, *"Get away from there. Move away."* At that time, you have shown what is more important; what is more valuable. You have said, *"I like that 23 year old boy on the TV who is going to take the free kick more than you."* Believe me, you cannot marry any of the people you see on TV. **You are only married to the one who is in flesh and blood with you so if you love your marriage, switch off the TV.**

How much time you spend with each other. How much time you spend listening to each other and talking with each other, doing things together, taking a stroll together, eating at a table together. It is quality time. It is time for you to eat. You just go, pick your plate and dish your food. You go and sit down in a corner and munch your food. Then your wife too goes, dishes hers, comes and munches hers as well. Why did you not just sit together and spend five minutes or ten minutes just eating together? **You may not talk much but it is called quality time and there is no interruption at that time.**

In that time, you may not argue but discuss interesting things about your life and that is about it - quality time. In this day and age, we all do not have the time. **You may not be able to spend an hour or three hours but five minutes or ten minutes of undivided attention that is quality time.** So the second language of love is spending quality time. The language of time. *"I want to be with you. Let us go out together. Let us go for dinner. Let us go for lunch. Let us go and stroll. Let us watch this movie together. Let us do this together."* **When you show quality time, you show the value of the person because you are choosing them over something that is also important.**

You also show priority and you give attention. Quality time is about prioritization. What is important? What is number one? What is valuable? I know, for all of us, in this day and age, are very busy. The men are busy. The women are busy. Everybody is working. Everybody has a high demand on their time in the office. Everybody has to finish assignments. **Everybody has to work with deadlines and all of us are working hard but if we are not careful, we may spend quality time with people we work with and not quality time with people we are married to and that will undermine any serious relationship.**

Quality time is not for you when you are married but also for the children. Quality time is for each other before you even marry. If you do not have time for each other, you cannot make time and cannot sacrifice time, then your love is not being communicated clearly. You may love but you are not communicating it. So that is the second language - spending quality time together.

Chapter Three

GIVING GIFTS

Third language of love – **giving gifts.** *For God so loved the world that He gave His only begotten Son...* **If you love, you give because affirmation is important, quality time is important as well as giving of gifts.** That is why in a wedding there is giving. The man gives a ring, the woman also gives a ring because **marriage is about giving and giving things which are valuable.** I know that all of us have grown up in different environments and you cannot blame people for the environment they grew up in.

You can only hold them accountable for their inability to take charge of their own lives after they have grown up to the age of accountability and responsibility but sometimes people grow up in an environment where giving is not practiced and there is no generosity. They do not know how to give and when they give, they feel pain.

Nonetheless, people sometimes grow up in environments where they give under different arrangements. People give to impress, not to show love so they will go out of their way to help somebody who is not really significant to them. Just somebody out there and take care of somebody but not their own. So you can have men who take care of other people's children and to those people, they are the best men in town but they do not take care of their own children. They will help somebody's wife solve their children's problems but never help their own wife to solve their children's problems.

They know how to give for showmanship but not to express love for the people who are important to them. So giving to your significant person is your spouse. If you are courting, it is the person whom you are beginning this journey, it is crucial to cement your love and giving does not have to be expensive. Giving has to be genuine though it has to be sincere but it does not have to be big necessarily. That does not mean that if you can afford big, you go and do small and say, *"Well, giving does not mean 'big'."* No but **little things which may not cost a lot of money will show affection.**

Remember the special days of your relationship. Birthdays. How do you feel if your wife forgets your birthday? How do you feel if your husband forgets your birthday? These birthdays are important. Most families in the past did not celebrate birthdays. Most of them grew up not knowing how to celebrate birthdays. You can imagine a man who has grown up in an environment where birthdays are not important, married to a woman, grown up in her family where they celebrate birthdays very, very purposefully. **The language of love will be problematic.**

It is important to remember special days. You do not have to forget birthdays. **Write down each other's birthday. Once you start courtship, remember birthdays. They are very important.**

Then you have to remember Christmas. It is the birthday of Jesus. Remember it because you have to do something. Remember occasions like New Year and Valentine's Day. Do not say, *"As for me, I do not celebrate Val's Day. As for me, I do not like*

Val's Day" especially if you are courting. You go and tell your girlfriend, *"I do not believe in Valentine. It is not in the Bible."* **The girl will leave you like that and you will say it is not in the Bible. Go and buy her something.**

So the special occasions are important. **If you are married, your wedding anniversary is very important. Do not forget your wedding anniversary.** Men, do not forget your wedding anniversary. There are people who live in Ghana, know when Chelsea is going to play Manchester United. They know when AC Milan is going to play San Dora. One of the things that amazes me during sports season when I see these young Ghanaians is that they know players and the goals they scored three years ago but cannot remember their girlfriend's birthday. **Where your heart is, there your memory is also. So remember the special occasion. Remember special days. Be generous and spontaneous.**

Giving must be spontaneous. Do things out of the blue. *"Oh, I went out, saw this and bought it for you." "I just bought you this." "I just bought you that." "I bought you lunch so that you do not cook today."* Words like that. **Some people think the language of love is I love you but so far as you can see, I have not said I love you because I love you is cheap.** *"Oh, I love you. You know I love you." "If you love me, show it." "You know my heart is yours. I love you."*

The language of love is not *"I love you."* It is not going out to say *"I love you."* **It comes in different ways. It is in giving.**

Chapter Four

ACTS OF SERVICE

Fourth language of love is in **the acts of service. Offering service.** What does it mean? It means **offering help to ease the burden of another person. You know somebody loves you when they make it easy for you to do your job; when they take the stress from you.**

If your wife is cooking on Saturday but you do not know how to cook. You just go, stand there, just pick the blender and blend the onions. You are doing something. Whiles your wife is cooking, you know after cooking she has to go to iron. So you go and iron so that after cooking she does not go and iron. **That is offering acts of service.**

You already know that he is tired and this responsibility is going to be difficult; just step in and make it easy for him. The child has been born and your wife has stayed up the whole night. Now she hears the baby crying; you know it is tough and you love to sleep too but for you to get up and say, *"You continue sleeping. I will continue to take care of the baby."* **That is love.** It is not saying, *"I love you! I love you!! I love you!!!"* **Pick the baby. That is love. Take the burden off.**

You know in this time and age most of us are stressed out, we go to work and we are stressed out but sometimes you may find one partner is stressed and the other has a little bit time. **Ease the**

stress of the other person. Carry some of the burden. Carry some of the responsibility. Go out of your way to do some things.

If you are a young couple and you have to pay bills, your office is closer to the billing office, you can easily go and pay. Do not say, *"Well, it is your job. Go and pay the bill."* When he has to drive across town to the billing office, you can just ease his burden. **It is called acts of service and when you do that for one another, it is love.**

I am not saying, *"Do not say 'I love you' "* but that act itself carries *"I love you"* on it and if you love people, you do things for them. **You do not make them work too hard and you know you are killing the woman but no sensitivity because you believe your woman must do this.** *"As for me, I do not like this."* **How much it hurts the person does not bother you. That is not love. That is dictatorship, bullying, tyranny and it is unfair because if it is done to you, you will not be happy especially for us men.**

We have to be more accommodating because you know the era when our mothers stayed at home and our fathers went to work are all over; by the time the man returned from work, the woman was at home, cleaned the house, washed the children's cloths and ironed them, cooked the food, set the food on the table, covered it with a lace. In those days, they served fufu in a Petri dish. Everything was set. Then the man comes just to sit down to finish the food. Sometimes he does not say thank you for the meal. He does not say how nice the meal was. He does not say, *"I appreciate it."*

He just eats it. He believes he has done his job. *"Your job is to cook; my job is to eat. Equal division of labor. I have finished my job."* Finishes it, leaves the plate behind, does not bother to wash his plate, he goes out, has his bath, picks new cloths and walks out. Those days are gone forever.

No modern day man can survive doing that. This time, you get home sometimes before your wife gets home because she is also working. She is also meeting deadlines just like you do. You went to university together. If you want the marriage I described, go to the bush. There are girls there. Go and marry them. They will say, *"Mewura! Mewura!! Mewura!!!"* **Now if you do not want that, then you have to change.**

When you marry those kinds of wives, you lock them in the room. Your friends do not see them. They know you are married but they never see her. When she comes out, chaos. **In this day, we have to support one another, we have to ease the burden of one another. When your wife supports you to make your work easy, you have to appreciate it. If your husband supports you to make the work easy, you have to appreciate him.**

If he goes out of his way when he sees you are busy and does something else so that you can relax, you have to appreciate it – vice versa – because we are all helping one another and sometimes the load becomes too heavy for either one of us and we have to act and offer service.

Chapter Five

PHYSICAL TOUCH

The fifth language of love is **physical touch.** What is physical touch? **Physical touch is showing affection through your presence and through your touch. Not every touch is of love. Sometimes physical touch can be angry. Sometimes it can be manipulative.** As you can tell, not every kiss is love. Judas kissed Jesus but it was not love. **So when I talk about physical touch, I am not talking about physical emotion.** Going to kiss the woman and holding her in a certain way to say, *"I love you! I love you!!"*

It is being affectionate. How does it work?

It starts with eye contact. Before your hand moves, your eyes must move. If you cannot look into each other's eyes endearingly, lovingly and show affection through eye contact, either when you are in a room, your wife is there, you are there but you just give a glance and you know there is telepathy going on at this time.

The people here have no idea what we are saying but deep communication is going on. I think almost all couples know how to communicate. In the midst of a crowd, they can look and say so many things in just one look or one just little smile or one wink of an eye. That is physical contact – physical touch. You have to be able to communicate not just by holding.

I want to kiss you. *"Mwah."* The men, most of the time, do not have the patience. They would want to do what they want to do quickly but **you start with eye contact.**

You follow it up with physical affectionate contact – whether putting your arm around your partner, holding hands which I know most of us find it difficult to do. Most couples do not know how to hold hands. Just hold hands and walk comfortably. Have their arms around each other. In public there is no affection; at home there is no affection. No holding of hands. No touching and then lights out. I am not going to go too much into that. **So it is eye contact, affectionate contact and then there is intimacy. We should be able to communicate love through physical touch.**

CONCLUSION

Thus, five languages. Different people respond differently at various levels to all of these. For some people, giving gifts is number one expression of love for them. For some people, affirmation is number one. For some people, acts of service is number one. Different people respond differently. Although all these are expressions of love, different people respond differently. That is why sometimes you know people can hate each other and still be sleeping with them. You can find couples who are struggling, fighting – the marriage is not working – but the wife is pregnant and sometimes when you see the pregnancy, you will think, *"Oh, they have solved their problems."* **They have not solved their problems because the language of love is not just physical touch.**

There are so many other issues that may not have been resolved. That is why you do not also use sex to solve problems because if you do that, you are avoiding the problem. It starts with affirmation. If you are constantly insulting each other, you are not solving the problem as you are having sex. You have to learn to show respect and you start with affirmation.

You have to spend quality time and I want to encourage all marriage couples, especially those of you who are yet to marry. Start right with quality time and do not allow interferences in your quality time whether they come from relatives or whatever. Set time aside to spend time with each other.

Learn to do things together. If you like exercise, you exercise together. You share the time together. If you like watching movies, you watch movies together. If you like reading, read together. If you like going out to the beach, you go together. Learn to do things together and share those moments together.

If you have a car, take time and drive. Just take a ride. Going nowhere. Not every trip must end at a destination. Some trips are to create time. Move out of Accra. Drive to some of the quiet areas; some of the quiet streets and roads. Drive safely. Go and stand by a village somewhere and just watch the life there. Enjoy quietness for a moment. Then you get back in your car and drive back home. **It does not cost money but it is quality time.**

One of the things you are going to notice when you are couples is when the children come. Quality time becomes difficult because they also need time. When you have one child, they can take all the time. When you have two, it is more time. It is difficult to make quality time because whilst you are making time, the children are crying, *"I need food. This one has taken my shoe and I am going to beat her."*

Sometimes it may mean you have to leave children somewhere and go out. Invest a lot in your marriage. Make time for gifts. Make time for acts of service. Make time for physical contact. If you are not married, you start with eye contact, affectionate contact, holding hands and stop. You end there.

The day you come to the altar and say, *"You are married"* then you go and finish the rest. I hope that you have received wisdom nuggets that will help you in your relationship. **Determine that this year, every word out of your mouth will be words of affirmation.** Amen.

Notes

Notes

Other Books by
Benjamin Osei Kuffour JNR

Treasures of Wisdom

The Making of a King